MW00426241

What I Love about Our Family

I love eating

_____

together.

Other people always seem
impressed that our family

_____ .

3

I love our family's unique way of celebrating

_____.

I love how we never get tired of

telling stories about

_____.

5

I love when

_____

wears

_____ .

6

I love going

_____

together.

I used to pretend our

_____

was a

_____.

8

I love how we are more

_____

than most families.

9

I love how we are less

_____

than most families.

10

I love all our different interests
and hobbies, like

_____

and

_____.

Being a part of this family gives
me a deep sense of

_____.

12

If we were superheroes,

our superpowers would be

_____.

13

Whenever I hear

———————————————————————————,

it always reminds me of our family.

14

I think our family brings a lot of

_____

to our neighborhood.

15

I love how

_____

always says,

" _____ "

16

Our family deserves the

_____

Award.

17

Our family would never win the

_____

Award.

18

I used to wish we weren't so

——————————————————————————————— ,

but now I'm glad.

19

I laugh every time I remember when we

_____ .

20

I love how we share simple things, like

_____ .

21

I hope we get to

_____

soon!

22

If we had a fairy godmother, I'd ask her
to grant us a lifetime supply of

_____

and

_____.

23

Being in this family has
probably made me a better

_____ .

24

Being in this family has probably

made me a worse

_____!

25

We would make the most

First Family in history.

26

I love how we share basic values, like

_____

and

_____.

27

Once and for all, I'd love to set
the family record straight about

_____ .

28

If they gave out medals for arguing about

————————————————————————,

we'd take home the gold.

29

I love hanging out in the

_____

and

_____

together.

30

The smell of

_____

always reminds me of

_____.

31

I love that our family still

_____ .

32

I love that we don't

———————————————

anymore!

33

Our holiday gatherings are always

_____ .

34

I'm glad I inherited

_____'s

knack for

_____.

35

One of my favorite family pictures

ever is the one from

_____ .

36

I love how the kids in this family

_____ .

37

I love how the grownups in this family

_____ .

38

I would love it if we could go to

_____

for a family reunion.

39

I love how our family proves

it's possible to be

_____

and

_____.

40

I love that our family seems to

have really good luck with

_____ .

41

Too bad we have such lousy luck with

_____!

42

I love to be able to watch our family

_____.

43

If I had to describe our family

in one word, it would be

" _____ "

44

One of my happiest family memories is

_____ .

It's nice that we all pretty much agree on

_____.

46

It's funny that we all
pretty much disagree on

_____ .

47

Maybe one day we'll stop teasing

_____

about

_____.

48

If our family were in charge of

——————————————————————————————— ,

the world would be a

———————————————————————————————

place.

49

I really depend on our family's

_____ .

50

I'm so

_____

we're a family.

I Love
Our Family!

Created, published, and distributed by Knock Knock
1635 Electric Ave.
Venice, CA 90291
knockknockstuff.com
Knock Knock is a registered trademark of Knock Knock LLC
Fill in the Love is a registered trademark of Knock Knock LLC

ISBN: 978-168349003-6
UPC: 825703-50258-9
10 9 8 7 6 5 4

#fillinthelove

Marshalls.

1281 - 090868346-000199- 22 -2
COMPARE AT
$3.00 $1.99

8192 -- 9225 -- 209720 -- 81